SPECTACULAR SPACE SCIENCE

Exploring
PLANET EARTH
AND THE MOON

Nancy Dickmann

rosen publishing's
**rosen
central**

New York

Published in 2016 by The Rosen Publishing Group, Inc.
29 East 21st Street
New York, NY 10010

Produced for Rosen by Calcium
Editors for Calcium: Sarah Eason and Jennifer Sanderson
Designer: Greg Tucker
Consultant: David Hawksett

Library of Congress Cataloging-in-Publication Data

Dickmann, Nancy.
Exploring planet Earth and the moon/Nancy Dickmann.—First edition.
    pages cm.—(Spectacular space science)
Includes bibliographical references and index.
ISBN 978-1-4994-3625-9 (library bound)—ISBN 978-1-4994-3627-3 (pbk.)—
ISBN 978-1-4994-3628-0 (6-pack)
1. Moon—Juvenile literature. 2. Earth (Planet)—Juvenile literature. I. Title.
QB582.D53 2016
523.3—dc23
                                                                    2014049472

Chapter One
Our Home Planet 4

Chapter Two
Beliefs About
the Moon 10

Chapter Three
Exploring the Moon 16

Chapter Four
What We Know
About the Moon 24

Chapter Five
Moon and Earth
Together 32

Chapter Six
What's Next? 38

Glossary 46

For More Information 47

Index 48

OUR HOME PLANET

Earth is an amazing place. It is covered with lush rain forests, craggy mountains, deep seas, and frozen ice caps. Most places on the planet are teeming with life, from the tiniest bacteria to the tallest trees—and, of course, humans, too. We are so used to Earth and its wonders that sometimes it is hard to remember that Earth is just one of the millions of planets scattered throughout the universe.

Not all planets are created equally. Earth is a rocky planet like Mercury, Venus, and Mars. Many larger planets (including Jupiter and Saturn) are made of gas, with no solid surface. Earth has a hard crust that surrounds it. Compared with the other layers of Earth, the crust is extremely thin: about twenty to thirty miles (thirty-two to forty-eight kilometers) thick on land and three to six miles (4.8 to 9.6 km) thick beneath the oceans. Beneath the crust there is a dense mantle of hot rock that can behave like a thick liquid. At the center is an iron core that is solid in the middle but liquid where it meets the mantle.

Earth's surface is home to many different environments, each providing a habitat for different types of plants and animals.

If you could peer beneath Earth's surface, you would see concentric layers of different materials.

HOW DO WE KNOW?

No one has ever been beneath Earth's crust. The deepest hole ever drilled went only about 7.6 miles (12.2 km) into Earth's crust—about 25 to 30 percent of the way to the mantle. So how do we know what is below the crust? One method for figuring it out is by studying the way that seismic waves from earthquakes travel through Earth. The waves travel at different speeds, depending on the material that they are traveling through, and measuring them helps scientists make predictions about what lies beneath the crust.

Earth's crust is broken up into large chunks called tectonic plates, a little like a giant jigsaw puzzle. These plates "float" on top of the mushy mantle, and although they move very slowly, their edges are constantly bumping and rubbing against each other. Where this happens, earthquakes and volcanoes are common. In some places, the plates are being pushed together, and in other places, they are moving apart.

Earth's Atmosphere

One thing that makes Earth so special is its atmosphere, made up of a mixture of gases that surround the planet like a blanket. Without the atmosphere, life could not exist. The atmosphere contains the oxygen that humans and other animals need to breathe, as well as the carbon dioxide that most plants need to make their food. It protects us from some of the sun's harmful radiation, and it traps the sun's heat, keeping the temperature fairly consistent. The atmosphere is also responsible for our weather, and it helps protect the surface from meteorite impacts and other objects from space. One of its only downsides is that it obscures our view of outer space, which is why we launch telescopes into orbit, where they have a clearer view.

Nearly all of Earth's weather, from gentle breezes to raging thunderstorms, takes place in the troposphere—the layer closest to the surface.

THIS PLACE HAS NO ATMOSPHERE

We are lucky to have our atmosphere. Mercury has practically no atmosphere at all, leaving it unprotected. Mercury's surface is pockmarked with craters caused by objects crashing into it. With no atmosphere to redistribute heat, the planet is boiling hot during the day and freezing at night. Mars also has a very thin atmosphere, leading to similar problems. Although there is frozen water in its crust, the lack of atmospheric pressure means that it cannot have liquid water on the surface.

Weather balloons are used every day around the world. They measure temperature, humidity, air pressure, and wind speed, and send the data back to a weather station on the ground.

The atmosphere is about three hundred miles (482 km) thick, but most of the mass in it is within about ten miles (16 km) of the surface. The farther up you go, the thinner the atmosphere becomes. Most of the matter—about 78 percent—is nitrogen. Oxygen makes up 21 percent of the atmosphere, and argon, carbon dioxide, water vapor, and other gases make up the remaining 1 percent.

Earth's atmosphere is divided into five main layers. Closest to the surface is the troposphere. It is about four to twelve miles (6.4 to 19.3 km) thick, and it is where most of our weather takes place. Above that is the stratosphere, where jet airplanes fly. Combined with the mesosphere, it forms the middle atmosphere. Above this level are the thermosphere and the exosphere. Scientists use many different methods to study the atmosphere, including radar, satellites, weather balloons, and other tools.

7

Magnetic Field

It is not just the atmosphere that surrounds Earth. Our planet's magnetic field cannot be seen or touched, but it plays just as important a role in protecting life on Earth. It is like a giant force field that protects the planet from the sun's radiation. The sun emits a stream of charged particles called the solar wind that travels out into the solar system. Earth's magnetosphere deflects the solar wind and protects the planet. If Earth did not have it, things would be very different. For example, Mars's magnetic field is so weak that it cannot prevent the solar wind from stripping away the planet's atmosphere.

Scientists believe that Earth's magnetic field is generated by movements in the liquid part of the planet's core. The inner and outer core spin at different rates, and this creates what is called the dynamo effect, causing Earth to behave like a huge electromagnet. Just like a magnet, it has two poles: north and south.

This diagram illustrates how Earth's magnetosphere (shown in blue) deflects the solar wind (shown in yellow).

The farther north you go (or south, in the Southern Hemisphere), the more likely you are to see an aurora.

AURORAS

From time to time, shimmering lights illuminate the areas in the far north and far south of the planet. These are the auroras, also known as the Northern Lights or Southern Lights. Long ago, the Vikings believed that the aurora was a fiery bridge to the sky, built by the gods. Scientists now know that the auroras are caused when a large blast of solar particles hits Earth. The particles interact with Earth's magnetosphere and atmosphere, causing the brilliantly colored lights.

Earth has a north and south pole at the ends of Earth's axis, the imaginary line that goes through the center of the planet. However, the magnetic north and south poles are not located along Earth's axis. They do not stay in one place, either—they "wander" by about twenty-five miles (40 km) per year. Once in a long while, the poles flip; the last time this happened was 780,000 years ago. Sometimes, large earthquakes can also change the magnetic field. Scientists are still trying to figure out exactly how changes deep within Earth can affect the magnetic field.

9

Chapter Two

BELIEFS ABOUT THE MOON

Aside from the sun, the moon is the biggest and brightest object in the sky. For thousands of years, early peoples watched the moon, marking the passage of time as it waxed and waned. It takes about 29.5 days for the moon to complete one orbit of Earth, and this formed the basis of many early calendars—the English word for "month" comes from "moon." Although the modern Western, or Gregorian, calendar does not strictly follow the lunar cycle, some calendar systems, including the Islamic calendar, do.

Many early cultures linked the moon with a god or goddess. For the ancient Greeks, the moon represented Artemis, the twin sister of Apollo. She was also the goddess of the hunt and she had a fierce temper. For the Fon people of Benin, the goddess Mawu represented the moon. She was also the goddess of night, joy, and motherhood.

To the ancient Romans, the moon was represented by Diana, who was also the goddess of the hunt and of childbirth.

In some cultures, stories about the moon are told to explain its behavior. For example, the Inuit of North America saw the sun and moon as brother and sister. The god Anningan was the moon, and the goddess Malina was the sun. Every month, Anningan became thinner and thinner as he chased Malina across the sky, forgetting to eat. Then, during the new moon, he disappeared to eat before returning to start the chase again. Malina wanted to evade her brother so the moon and sun would rise and set at different times.

FULL MOON

The full moon is given many different names throughout the year. For example, a full moon in the fall is often called a "Harvest Moon." This is because farmers can stay out late, harvesting their crops by its light. The Algonquian peoples of North America had a different name linked to nature and the seasons for the full moon each month. For example, June's moon was the "Strawberry Moon," because strawberries were ready to be picked, and November was the "Beaver Moon," because it was time to set beaver traps before the swamps froze.

The Ziggurat of Ur is one of many temples around the world that is dedicated to a moon god, in this case the Sumerian god Nanna. It was reconstructed in the 1980s.

The Moon in Culture

Throughout history, the moon has inspired many stories and legends. Many of them are based on the idea that the moon can affect events and people's behavior on Earth. For example, many cultures associate the full moon with unusual or dangerous behavior, such as sleepwalking and committing suicide or violent acts. Doctors and other professionals really believed that there was a strong link between madness and the full moon. In eighteenth-century England, people on trial for murder were sometimes given a lesser sentence if the crime happened during a full moon, the idea being that the moon made them do it. Our words "lunatic" and "lunacy" come from Luna, the Roman goddess of the moon.

There are many beliefs and superstitions linking the moon to weather on Earth. For example, one widespread belief is that when a new moon falls on Monday, good weather will follow. Another is that a reddish moon predicts wind. Although the moon does cause tides, so far there is no proof that it causes any other significant changes in the weather.

People have suggested that the moon's gravity, which pulls on Earth's oceans and causes tides, has a similar effect on the liquids in our bodies. During a full moon, they say that pull is strongest, causing a change in people's behavior. The pull of the moon's gravity increases only when the moon is closer than usual to Earth, and that can happen during any phase, not just the full moon. There is no scientific evidence to show that crime figures or other statistics go up and down along with the lunar cycle.

WEREWOLVES

Many cultures tell stories about werewolves—people who turn into dangerous part-wolf creatures after being bitten by one. Some of the most famous stories involve the person transforming into a werewolf during the full moon, which is probably based on the beliefs linking the full moon to violence and madness. However, werewolves are a fairly recent invention. In most of the older stories, the werewolf transformation is triggered by other things.

Many different cultures have beliefs linking the moon, especially the full moon, with spooky occurrences and behavior.

Early Studies

In addition to all the myths and superstitions, thousands of years ago, there were also people studying the moon from a scientific perspective. The writings of the Greek astronomer Pythagoras (c. 570–c. 500–490 BCE) show that he understood that the moon was spherical. He also believed that the moon orbits Earth—though at the time, most people thought that everything revolved around Earth.

Another Greek, Aristarchus of Samos (c. 310–c. 230 BCE), was able to estimate the size of the moon in 270 BCE, based on the amount of time that it spends in Earth's shadow. He estimated it at 0.33 of Earth's diameter, which is not far off the actual figure of 0.27. Other ancient astronomers were able to track the moon's position so accurately that they could predict both solar and lunar eclipses.

Once telescopes were invented in the early seventeenth century, people were able to learn much more about the moon. Galileo (1564–1642) used his telescope to make detailed drawings of the moon's surface. As telescopes improved, the maps improved. Two German astronomers were able to use math to calculate the height of many of the moon's mountains in the 1830s.

Pythagoras is credited with some of the first scientific discoveries about the moon, and he is honored by having a crater on the moon named after him.

Early astronomers could not see the moon's craters as clearly as we can today, which led to confusion about what caused them.

GETTING IT WRONG

Before telescopes were invented, no one was quite sure what the light and dark patches on the moon were. The writings of Aristotle (384–322 BCE), which were widely believed, stated that all heavenly bodies were perfect spheres, so the idea that the markings were mountains and valleys went against this. Some people suggested that the moon acted like a giant mirror, reflecting shapes on Earth. Once telescopes were available for studying the moon, it became clear that it did actually have mountains, craters, and valleys.

Mountains and valleys were easy to understand because they were similar to geographical features on Earth. However, craters were a different matter, and no one knew what caused them. Galileo thought that they were volcanic, and other theories included circular glaciers and coral atolls. It was only in the twentieth century that they were proven to be caused by impacts from other objects.

15

Chapter Three

EXPLORING THE MOON

In the 1950s, the United States and the USSR were locked in what is known as the Cold War. This conflict was not a war waged with weapons, but rather an intense competition between two different cultures: the capitalism of the United States and the communism of the Soviet Union. Each country turned to science to prove that its way was best, and billions of government dollars were pumped into scientific research, including space travel.

Early attempts to reach the moon were unsuccessful. The National Aeronautics and Space Adminstration's (NASA's) Pioneer program and the Soviet Union's Luna program both experienced several launch failures. Finally, in 1959, Luna 1 flew within about 3,700 miles (5,955 km) of the moon. That same year, Luna 2 became the first spacecraft to reach the moon's surface, and Luna 3 sent back the first photographs of the far side of the moon, which is never visible from Earth.

When Surveyor 3 landed on the moon in 1967, it conducted tests to see how the surface would cope with a larger spacecraft carrying astronauts. Two years later, Apollo 12 astronauts visited its landing site and took this photograph.

Meanwhile, with the exception of Pioneer 4, which reached a point about 37,300 miles (60,000 km) from the moon, NASA's spacecraft were failing one after the other. Finally, they began to catch up. In 1964 and 1965, three successful Ranger probes sent back thousands of photographs of the lunar surface. NASA scientists used these in their planning for manned missions.

In 1966, the Soviet Union achieved another first when it successfully put Luna 10 into orbit around the moon. NASA's Lunar Orbiter 1 was only a few months behind. Mastering this technique was crucial, because any crewed mission to the moon would require an orbiting spacecraft.

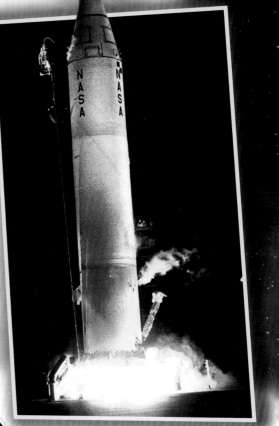

SOFT LANDINGS

In order to design a spacecraft that could safely land humans on the moon, scientists needed more than just photographs—they needed detailed data about the moon's surface. For example, they needed to know if a lander would sink into the dust on the surface, or break through the crust. In 1966, Luna 9 achieved the first soft landing on the moon, and NASA's Surveyor 1 managed it just four months later. Earlier spacecraft had been destroyed when they crashed into the moon, but these soft landers sent back extremely useful data.

When Pioneer 4 blasted off on March 3, 1959, it became the first U.S. probe to successfully escape Earth's gravity.

The Apollo Program

The early unmanned spacecraft increased our knowledge about the moon. For example, they sent back data about interplanetary gases, radiation levels on the moon, and its weak magnetic field. However, one of their main objectives was to help scientists prepare for a crewed mission to the moon. For example, from its position in orbit around the moon, Lunar Orbiter 1 sent back high-quality images of several potential landing sites. Other spacecraft, both U.S. and Soviet, analyzed the soil and tested for radioactivity.

By 1968, both countries were just about ready to attempt sending people to the moon. The USSR had successfully returned unmanned Zond probes to Earth after orbiting the moon. Then, in December 1968, NASA launched Apollo 8, and its crew of three became the first humans to travel to the moon. They completed ten orbits before returning to Earth. A few months later, Apollo 9 tested several technologies from low Earth orbit, including the lander's engines, life support systems, and docking maneuvers. Then in May 1969, Apollo 10 went into lunar orbit, and tested procedures for the first landing. Everything seemed to be working, and the stage was set.

On July 16, 1969, Michael Collins (b. 1930), Neil Armstrong (1930–2012), and Edwin "Buzz" Aldrin (b.1930) blasted off into space. After they entered orbit around the moon, the world held its breath while the Lunar Module detached from the rest of the craft and descended to the moon's surface. Finally, Armstrong stepped onto the moon's surface, uttering the famous words, "That's one small step for man, one giant leap for mankind."

TESTING THE SURFACE

In 1967, NASA's Surveyor 6 spacecraft successfully landed on the moon. After it touched down, its engines were fired to lift it about ten feet (three meters) off the surface and then touchdown a few feet away. Then it took photographs of its original landing site, looking to see if its rockets' exhaust had created a crater. There was no crater, which meant that the moon's surface must be solid and—hopefully!—safe for astronauts to land on.

Neil Armstrong took this famous photograph of Buzz Aldrin on the surface of the moon. You can see Armstrong and the Lunar Module reflected in Aldrin's visor.

Astronauts in Action

The Apollo 11 astronauts stayed on the moon's surface for about twenty-one hours. During that time, they deployed a solar-powered device containing a set of scientific instruments. The device could measure seismic activity and properties of the surface. The astronauts also collected rock samples to take home for analysis. When they landed back on Earth, they were greeted as heroes.

Five additional crewed missions landed on the moon. Like Apollo 11, each one consisted of a command module manned by one astronaut, which remained in orbit, and a Lunar Module crewed by two astronauts, which landed on the surface to explore and conduct experiments. The Apollo 12 astronauts collected samples and took readings of the solar wind, the magnetic field, the atmosphere, and other things. They also visited the Surveyor 3 spacecraft, which had made a soft landing two years before. They brought back some of its parts to examine on Earth.

This ordinary-looking box is one of the most useful tools set up on the moon by the Apollo astronauts. Scientists on Earth bounce lasers off this reflector, allowing them to measure the moon's distance with pinpoint accuracy.

Apollo 16's Lunar Roving Vehicle (LRV) traveled more than sixteen miles (26 km), although it never went more than 2.8 miles (4.5 km) from the Lunar Module. The astronauts had to be able to walk back if the LRV failed.

SOVIET SUCCESS

Although the Soviet Union never succeeded in landing a cosmonaut on the moon, it did continue to bring back new data. In the 1970s, three Luna spacecraft were able to return samples of moon rocks and dust to Earth. They also sent two successful robot rovers to explore the moon's surface: Lunokhod 1 in 1970 and Lunokhod 2 in 1973. The first traveled more than six miles (9.6 km) and sent back twenty thousand photographs. The second covered about four times the distance and took four times as many photographs.

Apollo 13, in 1970, was nearly a disaster. An onboard explosion made the astronauts abort the mission, but they managed to return safely to Earth. After a gap of nine months, Apollo 14 successfully landed on the moon. Apollo 15 made history by bringing along a LRV, which the astronauts could drive across the lunar terrain. This allowed them to cover a much wider area during the time they had on the moon. Apollo 16 and 17 followed in 1972, each with their own LRV and set of scientific tools. Since then, no one has visited the moon.

21

Recent Exploration

After the Apollo missions, interest in the moon waned, and scientists turned to other areas of research. Sending humans to the moon was expensive and dangerous, and there was a limit to how much they could learn. There were other exciting things to learn by studying other bodies in the solar system, as well as developing Earth-orbiting space stations such as Skylab, and new forms of transportation such as the space shuttle.

However, studying the moon has not been completely abandoned by scientists, and improved technology means that we can learn more about it than the Apollo astronauts could. In 1990, the Japanese Hiten spacecraft entered orbit around the moon, where it tested out various technologies. In the late 1990s, NASA's Lunar Prospector probe orbited the moon to search for water ice and other minerals. It was also able to map the composition of the moon's surface. The European Space Agency (ESA) launched its first lunar orbiter in 2003.

Ende

United States

After the Apollo program, NASA developed the space shuttle. It was designed to carry crew and cargo into orbit around Earth, where they could conduct scientific experiments.

The Lunar Prospector spacecraft was 4.5 feet (1.3 m) in diameter, and it was equipped with scientific tools for studying the moon.

A GLOBAL EFFORT

In the 1950s and 1960s, space exploration was dominated by the United States and the Soviet Union. However, exploring the moon—and the rest of space—is now a truly international endeavor. For the past several decades, ESA has been bringing together the top space scientists from around Europe, and the Japanese Aerospace Exploration Agency (JAXA) has been conducting its own research. India's Chandrayaan-1 spacecraft, consisting of an orbiter and lander, successfully studied the moon in 2008 and 2009.

JAXA launched Kayuga in 2007. Its tools included a high-definition television camera for sending back crystal-clear images, as well as a variety of other tools. China entered the field with Chang'e 1 in 2007. This spacecraft was able to create a highly accurate 3D map of the lunar surface, as well as analyze the chemical makeup of the surface and studying the impact of solar activity on Earth and the moon. Recent and current missions have discovered water ice on the moon, as well as some unbelievably cold areas in deep craters.

Chapter Four

WHAT WE KNOW ABOUT THE MOON

Decades of study with telescopes, probes, and crewed missions have meant that we probably know more about the moon than we do about any other object in space. We know, for example, that it is made up of concentric layers, similar to Earth. The rocky outer crust is about forty miles (64 km) deep, and below that there is a mantle about 620 miles (1,000 km) thick. At the center is a metallic core about 310 miles (500 km) wide.

Scientists have figured this out by using the same technique used to study Earth's internal structure: measuring seismic waves and analyzing how they pass through the moon. Tremors called "moonquakes" take place on the moon, but they are very weak compared with earthquakes. Impacts from meteorites also cause tremors. Instruments placed on the moon's surface still record vibrations, giving scientists the data they need.

The rock samples brought back by Apollo astronauts have been studied in great detail. This one weighs about fourteen pounds (6.3 kilograms).

Is the moon the result of a large object smashing into Earth?

WHERE DID THE MOON COME FROM?

The moon may have been created at the same time and from the same material as Earth, back in the early days of the solar system. It might have formed when a small planet collided with Earth, creating a huge cloud of rocky debris. This debris would have gradually clumped together to form the moon. Or it might have formed somewhere else and then been captured by Earth's gravity. Rocks brought back by the Apollo missions are slightly different from Earth rocks, so this supports the impact theory, but it is not yet completely proven.

Rock samples brought back from the moon have been useful in many ways. The mix of elements found in moon rocks suggests that the moon was once heated to very high temperatures. Some types of elements are radioactive and decay over time, at a very regular rate. By taking precise measurements of the amount of these elements found in a rock sample, scientists can calculate how old the rock is. Tests on moon rocks have shown that some of them are 4.4 billion years old.

The Moon's Surface

Early telescope users, such as Galileo, were able to see features on the moon's surface. There were dark, flat areas and jagged mountains, as well as deep canyons and circular craters. As telescopes improved, astronomers were able to make increasingly accurate maps of the moon's surface. When robotic probes started visiting the moon, we learned even more.

We now know that the moon's dark, flat areas (called *maria*, after the Latin word for "sea") were formed billions of years ago, when lava flowed across the moon's surface. They cover about 15 percent of the moon's surface and are much younger than other parts of the moon. In contrast, the brighter areas are known as highlands, or "terrae." NASA's Clementine spacecraft confirmed that the highlands are, on average, about 3.7 to 4.8 miles (6 to 7.7 km) higher than the maria.

The moon's maria got their name when early astronomers mistook them for actual oceans. They appear dark because their rocks are high in iron.

The moon's highlands are rough, mountainous, and pockmarked with craters. The tiniest craters are microscopic, and the largest is about 180 miles (290 km) across. Evidence from the Apollo missions proved that they are caused by meteorite impacts.

All of these features on the moon's surface are covered with a layer of fine powder and rubble anywhere from three to sixty feet (0.9 to 18 m) deep, called regolith. The regolith has been built up over billions of years by the debris of meteorite impacts, as well as cosmic dust that lands on the moon. The meteorite impacts mix the soil from different areas of the moon's surface. When samples of lunar soil are analyzed, they often include rock fragments from hundreds of miles away.

This may be one of the most famous footprints ever. Buzz Aldrin's boot left this impression in the moon's regolith.

ALREADY HERE?

When NASA scientists examined the rocks brought back by the Apollo astronauts, some of the results looked rather familiar. The scientists realized that moon rocks had already been discovered, right here on Earth! They had been blasted from the moon's surface by impacts from meteoroids and had fallen as meteorites. At the time they were found, no one had realized that they came from the moon. Lunar meteorites are extremely rare—only about one hundred have been discovered.

Water on the Moon?

Water is necessary for all life on Earth, and so far Earth is the only place we know of where liquid water exists on the surface. The temperature on Earth is ideal for water, and our atmosphere keeps it from evaporating into space. However, scientists have discovered frozen water in other locations around the solar system. This is a key area of research, since a source of water would be a huge benefit to any human settlement planned for the moon.

Scientists have known for a long time that liquid water could not exist on the surface of the moon. However, in the 1960s they began to speculate that ice might exist there, hidden from the sun's light in deep craters. In 1978, a team of Soviet scientists published research that showed traces of water in rock samples brought back by Luna 24. Spacecraft such as Clementine and Lunar Prospector tried to find evidence of frozen water, but did not come up with anything conclusive. The high-resolution imaging sensors on JAXA's Kayuga probe were unable to find any evidence of water in 2007.

Without the oceans and clouds constantly recycling water, life on Earth as we know it would not be possible.

In 2009 the LCROSS probe impacted the moon's south pole, creating a plume of debris that was analyzed by scientists. The scientists discovered more water than they had expected, though the moon's surface is still drier than any desert on Earth. Many scientists theorized that water on the moon came from comet or meteorite impacts, but new research suggests that it might have formed on the moon after exposure to the solar wind.

In this illustration you can see part of the LCROSS probe smashing into the moon's surface. The debris flung into the air by the impact was found to contain water ice.

SECOND TIME LUCKY?

When some of Apollo's rock samples were first analyzed, tiny traces of water were found, but scientists assumed that this was as a result of contamination on Earth. However, the rocks were examined again in the 2000s with more sensitive tools. Scientists found that the pebbles contained small amounts of water, and they were able to prove that the water had not been a result of contamination on Earth

Around the Moon

It is not just the moon's lack of oceans that sets it apart from Earth. The moon has virtually no atmosphere and no magnetic field. Both of these are crucial to life on Earth, so without their protection, life would be impossible on the moon.

The moon's atmosphere is extremely thin, about as dense as the outermost layers of Earth's atmosphere, where the International Space Station (ISS) orbits. Unlike Earth's atmosphere, where the atoms and molecules constantly collide with each other, the moon's atmosphere is so thin that its atoms and molecules almost never collide. It is made up of a mixture of gases, including some that are not found in Earth's atmosphere.

The LACE device, set up by the Apollo 17 astronauts, provided the first precise measurements of helium in the moon's atmosphere.

LEARNING ABOUT THE ATMOSPHERE

The Apollo 17 astronauts set up a tool called the Lunar Atmospheric Composition Experiment (LACE) on the surface in 1972. LACE was able to detect tiny amounts of elements and compounds such as helium, argon, neon, methane, and carbon dioxide. Since then, researchers on Earth have been able to use telescopes to detect sodium and potassium atoms in the moon's atmosphere by making images of the atoms' glow as they are energized by the sun.

When a magnet is placed near iron filings, they arrange themselves along the line of the magnetic field.

The moon contains very weak magnetism in its crust, but no dipolar magnetic field like Earth has. Data gathered by the Apollo missions showed that it had a stronger magnetic field in the past. The rock samples they brought back showed evidence of being magnetized. This is usually caused by the rocks being heated and then cooled down in a magnetic field. The metallic particles in the rock "freeze" along the lines of the magnetic fields, leaving a permanent record.

Where did this magnetic field come from, and why did it disappear? Unlike Earth's core, the moon's core is not magnetic. The magnetism of Earth is caused by convection currents in the liquid core, so if the moon's core is not magnetic, it probably has a solid core. The magnetized rocks suggest that the moon's core may have been liquid about 3.8 billion years ago.

Chapter Five

MOON AND EARTH TOGETHER

The moon is our closest neighbor in space, and we are able to see several of its features and behaviors in detail. One of these is the phases of the moon, as it appears to change shape over the course of a lunar cycle. Mercury and Venus have phases, too, but their orbits lie between Earth and the sun, so their phases cannot be seen with the naked eye. However, the moon's phases are easy to see.

Although the moon appears bright, it does not make its own light. Instead, it reflects light from the sun. Depending on where the moon is in its orbit of Earth, we see a different amount of it lit by the sun. For example, when the moon is on the opposite side of Earth from the sun, the sun's light illuminates its whole disc, and we see a full moon. When it is between Earth and the sun, its lit side is facing away from us, and it appears to disappear. When it is halfway between the two points, we see half of its lit face, giving it the appearance of a semi-circle.

Each lunar cycle, the moon goes from a thin crescent to a full moon, then back to a crescent again.

The far side of the moon looks quite different from the side we normally see. It has more craters and fewer maria.

LIBRATION

In spite of the moon's synchronous rotation, over a period of time we are able to see a little more than half of its surface—about 59 percent, in fact. This is due to a phenomenon known as libration. The moon has a slight "wobble" as a result of small variations in its rotation speed, which are caused by its elliptical orbit. When the moon is slightly closer to Earth, it moves faster than when it is farther away.

We always see the same side of the moon, but this does not mean the moon stays still. It rotates on its axis, just like Earth does, but it takes the same amount of time to rotate on its axis as it does to complete one orbit of Earth. This is called synchronous rotation, and many other moons in the solar system rotate in the same way.

33

Tides

The Earth has a huge influence on the moon and its force of gravity holds the moon in its orbit. However, the moon also influences conditions on Earth. It has its own gravity, and although it is weaker than Earth's, it still has an effect on our planet. When it pulls on Earth, it causes the side of it closest to the moon to "bulge" slightly. This effect is not really noticeable on land, but it is more dramatic at sea, and it is this that causes our tides.

Some coastal regions get two high tides each day, and others have only one. The angle of the moon's orbit causes this difference. The moon does not orbit directly around Earth's equator, so at any given time the maximum "bulge" of the ocean is usually either above or below the equator. Some areas on Earth experience only one of the tidal bulges in a day.

The moon orbits around Earth in the same direction that Earth rotates on its axis. This means that once the moon is in line with a particular point on Earth's surface, it takes nearly twenty-five hours to line up with that same point again. In an area that has two high tides each day, one high tide will come twelve hours and twenty-five minutes after the previous high tide.

SPRING TIDES

The sun's gravity also has an effect on tides, but since the sun is much farther away, its effect is not as strong as that of the moon's gravity. However, when the moon and sun are both in line with Earth, the force of their gravity is combined, and this creates a higher high tide than normal, called a spring tide. Midway between two spring tides we get a neap tide, where the sun and moon are pulling from different directions. The neap tide causes a smaller difference between high and low tides.

The difference in water level between high tide and low tide can be significant. Just a few hours after this photograph was taken, the boats were floating in the harbor.

Eclipses

The moon appears to disappear once a month, during the new moon phase. However, it can also nearly disappear for short periods at other times, when it is supposed to be full. This is called a lunar eclipse, and it happens when Earth moves directly between the sun and the moon, causing a shadow to cover the moon's surface.

Although Earth passes between the moon and the sun once in each lunar cycle, we get a lunar eclipse only when they line up just right. This can happen from two to four times in a single year. Unlike a solar eclipse, which can be seen from only a relatively small area on Earth's surface, everyone on the night side of Earth can see a lunar eclipse.

During a total lunar eclipse, the moon can turn a dark red color, giving it the name "blood moon."

During a partial eclipse, only part of the moon is blocked from view, but it has a different shape from one of its normal phases.

SOLAR ECLIPSES

Lunar eclipses are impressive, but solar eclipses are even more amazing. During a solar eclipse, the moon moves between the sun and Earth, and completely blocks the sun from some vantage points on Earth. The sun is about four hundred times bigger in diameter than our moon, but it is also about four hundred times farther away, so they appear almost exactly the same size in the sky. This makes the moon the perfect size to cover the sun. A total solar eclipse can cause darkness in the middle of the day.

The shadow that Earth casts on the moon has two parts: the umbra, or central region (where all of the sun's rays are blocked), and the penumbra, which is the outer region (where only some of the sun's rays are blocked). In a penumbral lunar eclipse, the moon passes through just the penumbra, and the visible effect on the moon is hardly noticeable. In a partial lunar eclipse, only part of the moon passes through the umbral shadow. These are easy to see, and the moon will look like it has a bite taken out of it. In a total lunar eclipse, the entire moon passes through the penumbra. It appears to change color until it goes almost completely dark.

37

Chapter Six

WHAT'S NEXT?

The past decade has seen a surge of renewed interest in the moon. In 2009, NASA launched the Lunar Reconnaissance Orbiter (LRO), which spent years making detailed maps in order to pave the way for astronauts to return to the moon. The data sent back by LRO can help identify possible landing sites by looking at the terrain, radiation, and usable resources within a specific location. LRO was joined in 2013 by the Lunar Atmosphere and Dust Environment Explorer (LADEE), which took readings of the moon's atmosphere and dust from orbit. The goal was to learn more about the behavior and effects of dust in the air, which may affect exploration and astronomy on the moon.

In 2013, the Chinese Chang'e 3 spacecraft became the first spacecraft since 1976 to soft-land on the moon. Its rover, named "Yutu," was unable to travel as far as was hoped, but it still managed to send back some useful data. The mission was planned as an intermediate step in China's moon exploration strategy. The first step was achieving moon orbit, which they did with Chang'e 1 and Chang'e 2. The third step is a sample return mission. India is also planning an orbiter and rover.

The LRO sent back a huge number of images, including some showing equipment left behind by the Apollo missions.

Top: The LRO took this photograph of peaks in the center of Tycho crater. The peaks are about 9.3 miles (15 km) wide in total, and the highest one rises 1.24 miles (2 km) from the crater floor.

Right: Some of LRO's images show volcanic deposits on the moon. These areas are probably the remains of small eruptions.

There have been many proposals for sending astronauts back to the moon. NASA drew up plans to work toward a crewed mission, but they were eventually shelved. The program would have been extremely expensive, and a decision was made to prioritize the Asteroid Redirect Mission instead. This project involves capturing a small near-Earth asteroid (NEA) and bringing it into orbit around the moon, where it will be studied in detail.

BACK IN THE HUNT

After early success, the Soviets pulled back from moon exploration in the 1970s. However, today, Russia is planning a return with two missions to the moon. Luna-Glob 1 will consist of an orbiter with ground-penetrating sensors, and Luna-Glob 2 will be made up of an orbiter as well as a lander and rover that will explore the south pole area.

39

Private Exploration

NASA has not completely given up on the moon. Instead, it is looking for ways to encourage private companies to take part in lunar exploration. In 2013, it established the Lunar Cargo Transportation and Landing by Soft Touchdown (CATALYST) program to help private companies develop robotic lunar landers. NASA will not provide any funding for the private companies, but it will offer technical advice and access to facilities and equipment.

Why are private companies interested in going to the moon? The Apollo program came out of a desire to increase our scientific knowledge, and to beat the Soviet Union in the space race. The current crop of private entrepreneurs trying to develop spacecraft have different motives. Some might be interested in opening up the moon to tourism; others want to set up mining operations and exploit its mineral resources. Others see the moon as the obvious next step for human settlement.

Building the ISS was a huge undertaking, and keeping its astronauts supplied is a big job. Private companies are taking over some of these tasks.

THE LUNAR XPRIZE

The Google Lunar XPrize was announced in 2007 as a way of encouraging innovation in space exploration. The challenge was simple: land a robot on the moon, make it travel more than 1,640 feet (500 m), and send back high-definition images and video. The first team to accomplish the mission will win $20 million, and the second place prize is $5 million. Other prizes are available to rovers that complete additional tasks. Entry was only available to teams that received fewer than 10 percent of their funding from government sources.

When the space shuttle program was terminated in 2011, NASA needed a new way to take crew and cargo back and forth to the ISS. They opened up cargo operations to private companies, believing that competition would lead to better prices. Two companies are now flying cargo missions to the ISS.

The Cygnus spacecraft, launched by Orbital Science Corporation, is one of two private spacecraft running cargo missions to the ISS.

Space exploration is difficult and expensive, even for a destination as close as the moon. National and international space agencies will always have a role to play. By working together with privately funded projects, they may be able to revolutionize space exploration.

41

Colonies on the Moon

Astronauts live on the ISS for months at a time. Could they live just as easily on the moon? For a long time, moon bases were a topic for science fiction, and not a realistic project. It is easy, however, to see why the idea is so attractive. The moon has valuable mineral resources, and it is also a useful place for doing science. Its lack of a thick atmosphere would make it an ideal site for telescopes, and scientists could carry out experiments in its low gravity.

Many scientists and designers have come up with suggestions of what a moon base might look like.

However, setting up a moon base would be challenging. To support a human population, we would need to recreate conditions similar to Earth. Human colonists would need air to breathe, water to drink, and food to eat. They would need to be protected from extreme temperatures, solar radiation, and low atmospheric pressure.

The moon has several advantages over other possible destinations, such as Mars. For one thing, it is very close. It took Apollo 11 about three days to reach the moon, but to get to Mars would take about six months. This means that transporting cargo and crew back and forth to the moon will be much easier. The discovery of water ice on the moon is also a positive sign. Astronauts could use this for drinking, as well as for making rocket fuel. The oxygen locked in the moon's soil could be harvested using heat and electricity to provide breathable air for the colonists.

WE NEED GRAVITY

Human bodies are not designed to cope without gravity. Astronauts who have spent several months on the ISS often need to be carried away on stretchers once they land back on Earth. This is because their muscles do not have to work as hard when they are weightless in space. Their muscles lose mass, and so do their bones. Astronauts on the ISS follow a carefully-designed fitness program to keep from losing too much muscle and bone mass. Any long-term residents of the moon's lower gravity would need to do the same.

New Ideas

The future of space exploration will depend on our ability to develop new technologies. A modern smartphone has more computing power than the spacecraft that took Neil Armstrong to the moon. New breakthroughs and discoveries are made every year that get us closer to the dream of exploring and colonizing space.

NASA and other space agencies are working on concepts and prototypes for a variety of new technologies. For example, there are scientists working on different systems of propulsion to make transporting astronauts and cargo cheaper and easier. Improved, more precise guidance and landing systems will make entering orbit and landing safer. It currently costs about $50,000 to send one pound of material to the moon, but new, lightweight materials could make spacecraft lighter, and therefore cheaper to launch.

If this prototype space habitat performs well during rigorous testing, it may be developed further for use by astronauts on the moon.

Astronauts often do their training and testing underwater, because working there is similar to working in the weightless conditions of space.

However, the spacecraft that will take astronauts to the moon is only one piece of the puzzle. Scientists are also working on more efficient ways to provide low-cost power for long trips as well as for settlements. Improvements to space suits will allow astronauts to explore and carry out research outside their base. Research continues into life-support systems that will allow humans to live on other worlds.

To test some of these new technologies, scientists conduct what they call "analog missions." These are tests in locations that are similar to the extreme environments of a space mission. For example, technology for spacewalks is often tested underwater, which makes for conditions similar to low gravity. Sand dunes in Washington state provide a good location for testing space suits and robotic rovers.

REAL MOONWALKS?

One promising new technology is the use of inflatable habitats to house moon colonists. NASA has tested a type of inflatable dwelling, similar to a carnival moonwalk, in the harsh conditions of Antarctica. If successful, these units would provide living space that could be insulated, heated, and pressurized. It would be fairly lightweight, so transporting it to the moon would not be difficult. It can also be taken down and re-used multiple times.

45

GLOSSARY

asteroid A small, rocky body that orbits the sun.

atmosphere The layer of gases surrounding a planet or moon.

atoms The smallest possible units of chemical elements.

aurora A glow in the upper atmosphere caused when charged particles from the sun interfere with Earth's magnetic field.

axis An imaginary line through the center of a planet, around which it rotates.

compounds Substances made up of two or more different elements that are bonded together.

convection A way of transferring heat in a liquid or gas, when warmer, less dense material moves upward and is replaced by cooler, denser material.

core The center area of something.

craters Hollow areas, like the inside of bowls, created when objects crash into planets or other large objects.

crust The hard outer shell of something.

elements Substances that cannot be separated into simpler substances.

equator An imaginary line that goes around the center of a planet or moon, halfway between its two poles.

gravity The force that pulls all objects toward each other.

lander A spacecraft designed to land on the surface of a planet or other object and send back data.

magnetic field The space around a magnet in which a magnetic force is active.

magnetosphere The region surrounding a planet or other object in which its magnetic field is the dominant magnetic field.

mantle The layer of Earth that lies between the crust and the core.

mass A measure of how much matter is in an object.

meteorite A lump of stone or metal from a meteor that has landed on Earth.

orbit The curved path that one body in space takes around another.

phase The apparent change in shape of the moon, Venus, or Mercury, as seen from Earth as they move in their orbits.

probes Instruments or tools used to explore something that cannot be observed directly.

radiation Waves of energy sent out by sources of heat or light, such as the sun.

rotates Spins around a central axis.

rovers Robot vehicles designed to travel across the surface of a planet or moon and collect data.

seismic waves Waves of energy generated by an earthquake or other event that travel within Earth or along its surface.

solar eclipse A phenomenon that occurs when the moon travels directly between Earth and the sun, blocking its light.

solar wind A flow of charged particles that travels out from the sun into the solar system.

tectonic plates The segments of Earth's crust that move around in relation to one another. Movement of tectonic plates causes earthquakes and volcanoes.

tides The regular change in the height of the surface of oceans and other bodies of water, caused by the pull of the moon's gravity.

universe All matter and energy that exist.

FOR MORE INFORMATION

Books

Aguilar, David A. *Space Encyclopedia: A Tour of Our Solar System and Beyond*. Washington, D.C.: National Geographic Kids, 2013.

Close, Edward. *Moon Missions* (Discovery Education: Earth and Space Science). New York, NY: PowerKids Press, 2014.

Einspruch, Andrew. *Mysteries of the Universe: How Astronomers Explore Space* (National Geographic Science Chapters). Washington, D.C.: National Geographic Children's Books, 2006.

Hunter, Nick. *Earth* (Astronaut Travel Guides). Chicago, IL: Heinemann-Raintree, 2012.

Mattern, Joanne. *Our Moon* (The Solar System and Beyond). Mankato, MN: Capstone Press, 2011.

Oxlade, Chris. *The Moon* (Astronaut Travel Guides). Chicago, IL: Heinemann-Raintree, 2012.

Websites

Due to the changing nature of Internet links, Rosen Publishing has developed an online list of websites related to the subject of this book. This site is updated regularly. Please use this link to access the list:

http://www.rosenlinks.com/SSS/Earth

INDEX

Aldrin, Edwin Buzz 18, 19, 27
Apollo (missions) 16, 18, 20, 21, 22, 24, 25, 27, 29, 30, 31, 38, 40, 43
Aristarchus of Samos 14
Armstrong, Neil 18, 19, 44
atmosphere 6–7, 8, 9, 20, 28, 30, 38, 42
aurora 9

carbon dioxide 6, 7, 30
Chandrayaan 23
Chang'e 23, 38
Clementine 26, 28
Collins, Michael 18
convection 31
core 4, 8, 24, 31
craters 7, 14, 15, 18, 23, 26, 27, 28, 33, 39
crust 4, 5, 7, 17, 24, 31
Cygnus 41

eclipses 14, 36–37
European Space Agency (ESA) 22, 23
exosphere 7

Galileo 14, 15, 26
gravity 12, 17, 25, 34, 42, 43, 45

Hiten 22

International Space Station (ISS) 30, 40, 41, 42, 43

Japanese Aerospace Exploration Agency (JAXA) 23, 28

Kayuga 23, 28

LCROSS 29
Luna 16, 17, 21, 28
Luna-Glob 39
Lunar Atmosphere and Dust Environment Explorer (LADEE) 38
Lunar Atmospheric Composition Experiment (LACE) 30
Lunar Cargo Transportation and Landing by Soft Touchdown (CATALYST) 40
lunar cycle 10, 12, 32, 36
Lunar Prospector 22, 23, 28
Lunar Reconnaissance Orbiter (LRO) 38, 39
Lunar XPrize 41
Lunokhod 21

magnetic field 8–9, 18, 20, 30, 31
magnetosphere 8, 9
mantle 4, 5, 24
maria 26, 33
Mars 4, 7, 8, 43
mesosphere 7
meteorite 6, 24, 27, 29
mountains 4, 14, 15, 26

National Aeronautics and Space Administration (NASA) 16, 17, 18, 22, 26, 27, 38, 39, 40, 41, 44, 45

oceans 4, 12, 26, 28, 30, 34
oxygen 6, 7, 43

phases of moon 32, 37
Pioneer program 16, 17
poles 8, 9, 29, 39
Pythagoras 14

radiation 6, 8, 18, 38, 43
Ranger 17
regolith 27

seismic waves 5, 24
Skylab 22
solar system 8, 22, 25, 28, 33
solar wind 8, 20, 29
Soviet Union 16, 17, 18, 21, 23, 28, 40
stratosphere 7
Surveyor 16, 17, 18, 20
synchronous rotation 33

tectonic plates 5
thermosphere 7
tides 12, 34–35
troposphere 6, 7

United States 16, 17, 18, 23

water 7, 22, 23, 28–29, 35, 43